Check out Violin Explained Etsy Merch !

https://www.etsy.com/shop/ViolinExplained

Vi·o·la (noun)

Violist:
a person who plays the viola.

Check out Violin Explained Etsy Merch Shop

https://www.etsy.com/shop/ViolinExplained

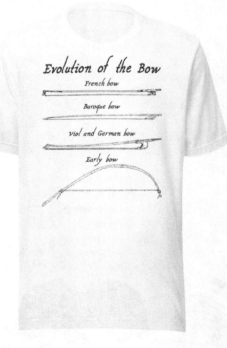

Learn Viola Fast - Book 2

Skills and knowledge you will learn:

- Intonation and what it means to play in tune
- Bow control and sound manipulation
- Muscle tension and body awareness
- The Sound Formula
- How to create meaning with sound
- Dotted rhythms and triplets
- String Crossing
- Bow direction, slurs, legato, staccato, tenuto.
- Playing with the pinky.
- Retakes, up bows, and hooked slurs.
- Playing with Low 2's

Songs and Pieces you will learn:

- Star Spangled Banner - USA National Anthem
- Minuet 1, 2, and 3 - J.S. Bach
- We Shall Overcome - American Spiritual
- Jana Gana Mana - India's National Anthem
- Nobody Knows the Trouble I've Seen - Spiritual
- Boat Song - Korean Folk Song
- Flower Drumbeats - Chinese Folk Song
- Original Pieces composed by Sergei
- Original Exercises and much more!

Dear Musician,

The Learn Viola Fast (Violin, Viola, Cello, and Bass) series is designed to assist both students and teachers in learning to play this beautiful instrument as quickly as possible. This resource can be used alongside any other methods or approaches to learning how to play a musical instrument. You are encouraged to go through the books as they are or jump around based on the student's needs and skip any parts that are not deemed necessary or appropriate for the situation and student. Based on the author's experience, the logic behind the books is as follows:

- Developing fine and gross motor skills to play the viola properly takes time.
- By learning all aspects of music and motion from the start, students develop a much better understanding of how to create beautiful music and are ready for more challenging skills later in their journey.
- Skills should be explained, practiced on simple exercises, then simple songs, followed by new materials and music.
- All basic skills of playing the viola should be learned as quickly as possible. This is accomplished by inclusion of explanations, diagrams, simple exercises, practiced on familiar music (such as folk songs like Twinkle), followed by newer, more challenging material.

Book 1 aims to teach as much of the mechanics of music and the body as possible, while the student is developing muscle strength to play for prolonged periods of time. Emphasis is placed on understanding how music and the viola work, while learning to pluck and play simple music with the bow.

Book 2 aims to ensure that the student is comfortable reading music and has the ability to create beautiful sound while maintaining control of muscle tension and good positions while playing. By increasing the difficulty of the left hand too quickly, bad habits such as excessive muscle tension and bad posture and hand positions proliferate, unnecessarily complicating the musician's journey down the line. If the student cannot play in tune, with good sound and tone, simple music with left fingers on the tapes, they should not move on to more challenging material. Hence the abundance of exercises and simple music in the first two books.

Book 3 aims to teach and introduce most skills that the student needs in order to play more challenging music, in a simple manner with explanations, simple music, and plenty of practice.

It is my deepest hope that these resources will help you make beautiful music and find joy in playing the viola.

Other books by Sergei

Complete scale series for all bowed string instruments that can be used in the orchestra classroom, as well as private studio environment.

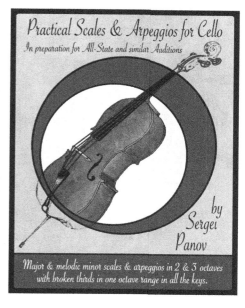

A music manuscript paper book that's easy to use with space for lots of notes. Perfect for every musician. Whether you're composing your own music or taking a music theory course, this book is great for all note notation needs. All books are available on Amazon.

Learn Violin, Viola, and Bass complete series (Bass coming soon)

Violin method is available in Spanish!

Please visit my youtube and social media channels, Violin Explained.
www.violinexplained.com

The text presented in this book was initially generated by the author, with assistance from GPT-4, OpenAI's sophisticated language-generation model. While all original content was created by the author, certain sections underwent proofreading and editing for improved readability by ChatGPT-4. The author then made additional edits and modifications to align the content with his preferences. It is important to note that the author retains full responsibility for the final text included in this book.

Photographer: Jessica Priscilla Caceda

So, you're interested in learning to play the viola? That's fantastic! You might have heard that it's really difficult and requires years of practice just to create beautiful sound. However, that's not true. Sure, if your aim is to become an expert with exceptional technical skills, it'll take 10,000 hours of focused practice with a top-notch teacher. But, you can learn to play the viola, produce beautiful sound, and most importantly, enjoy the process relatively quickly. All you need is a good-quality viola, the *Learn Viola Fast* method books, and a positive attitude along with a strong work ethic. Practicing a little bit but frequently will help you progress significantly. I know this method works because I've helped hundreds of students who now love playing the viola, have fun learning new music, and enjoy playing solo, in small groups, or in larger ensembles like youth and community orchestras.

To make this learning process effective, it's important to follow a specific order. First, you need to grasp some musical concepts and the mechanics of the viola so you can understand how everything works. If you skip this essential step, you might feel overwhelmed and frustrated when trying to learn more complex techniques like shifting and playing with flats and sharps, and you could even give up. I've seen this happen many times. This foundational knowledge is crucial for learning to play the viola well and quickly.

Each of the three Learn Viola Fast books contains detailed explanations, key highlights, visual diagrams, and quizzes to test your understanding. Images of specific steps and techniques visually demonstrate how to perform various tasks. When you understand the how and why behind each action, your body, hands, and fingers will more easily adapt to new and unfamiliar movements. Here's a summary of what you'll learn in each book:

- **Book 1** - Basics: You'll learn how music and the viola work, how to play simple songs, and how to understand music notation.
- **Book 2** - Right Hand: This book mainly focuses on using the bow to create beautiful sounds, altering sound to convey meaning, and playing with the second/middle finger.
- **Book 3** - Left Hand: You'll learn all about left finger placements, shifting, vibrato, chords, and more.

Are you prepared to learn one of the most enchanting instruments in the world? If so, join me on this exciting journey to learn the viola quickly!

Contents

Part I - Review

Before we dive into new skills, let's take a moment to review what you've learned in Book 1 by practicing these pieces.

Pluck the strings (pizzicato) and play with the bow (arco). Aim to memorize and practice the power of 10, which means playing the pieces ten times a day. Feel free to mix up your practice routine by plucking, copying and writing down the notes, and playing with the bow. To help with memorization, write down the note names from memory and try humming them too.

1. C string review

Cut Time - time signature.

It essentially tells you to count two half notes per bar, instead of 4 quarter notes.

The sum of the measure is the same (2/2 = 4/4) but the feel is different.

2. Rigadoon, H. Purcell - arr. Sergei Panov

Allegro

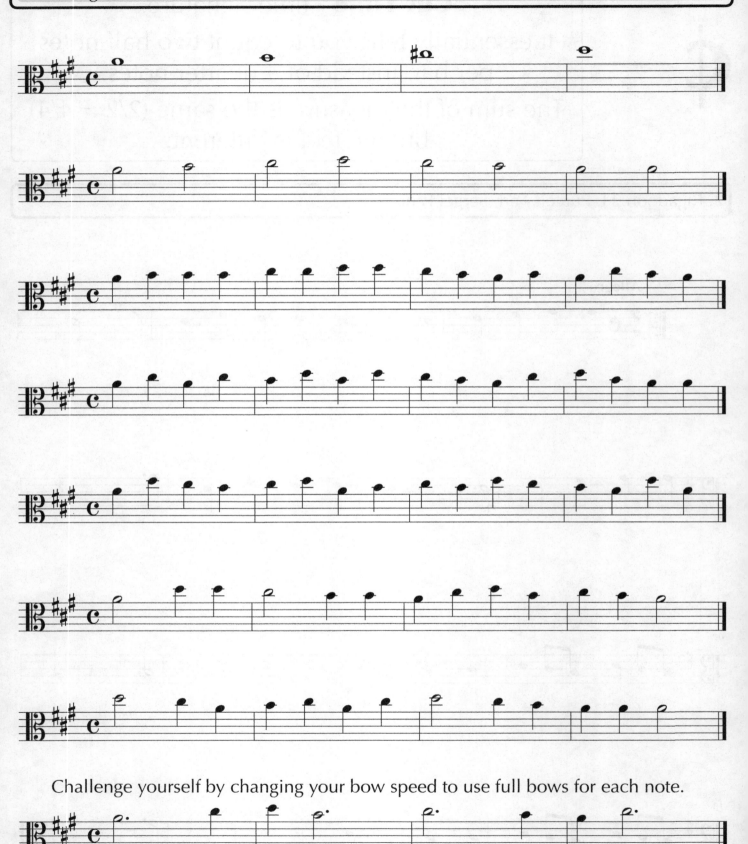

Challenge yourself by changing your bow speed to use full bows for each note.

4. Black Forest Waltz - German Folk Song, arr. Sergei Panov

Allegretto

Part II - Intonation

5. What does it mean to play in tune?

Up until now, we've been playing by placing our left-hand fingers on tapes. You know you're playing the correct note when the tip of your left-hand finger is on the tape.

? More advanced students and professionals don't use tapes, so how do they know where to place their fingers?

Remember from Book 1, Section 13, that a half step is 5% of the string's length, and a whole step is 10%. No two half or whole steps are exactly the same distance, as pressing your fingers down shortens the string, making the next 10% smaller.

You can roughly estimate the distance between notes. For example, the first tape is about three inches, the second tape is about two inches, and the third tape is about an inch from. But is there a more precise way to know?

Important Information

When you play certain notes in tune, the viola's open strings vibrate and ring. This is called forced vibration.

RULE!

Forced vibration happens when interconnected objects, like strings, are made to vibrate because they share the same fundamental frequency. The bridge is what connects the strings.

To practice forced vibration, play loudly with full bows to make the strings vibrate as much as possible. Keep your bow close to the bridge (in the highway or the sounding point) and ensure that your left-hand fingers are raised and curved, not touching any open strings.

When your left-hand finger is in tune, the corresponding open strings will vibrate due to forced vibration, as the strings are interconnected through the bridge. As we play, the bridge moves and vibrates. If the bridge's fundamental vibrations match those of the open strings, those strings will vibrate even if the bow isn't touching them.

Observe and listen to your viola and the open strings to notice the forced vibrations. Remember, forced vibrations equal playing in tune.

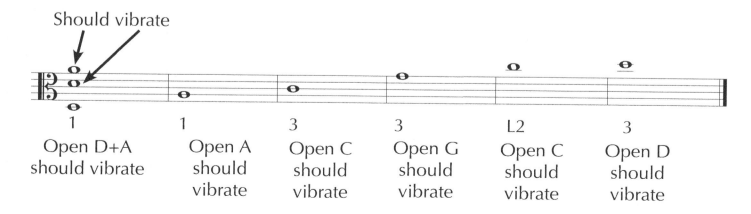

Should vibrate

1	1	3	3	L2	3
Open D+A should vibrate	Open A should vibrate	Open C should vibrate	Open G should vibrate	Open C should vibrate	Open D should vibrate

If you enjoy math, let's discuss some numbers.

Review Book 1 sections 1 and 2. Air vibrations (changes in air pressure) create the sounds we perceive. When a viola string is plucked or bowed, the body vibrates, sending vibrations through the bridge to the rest of the viola's body, causing it to shake, changing air pressure, and creating sound.

When you play an open A string, it vibrates 440 times per second, or Hertz (Hz). An open A has a frequency of 440 Hz. Here are the frequencies of the notes you encountered in the previous example (rounded to the nearest whole number for simplicity).

Notes on the viola with forced vibrations:

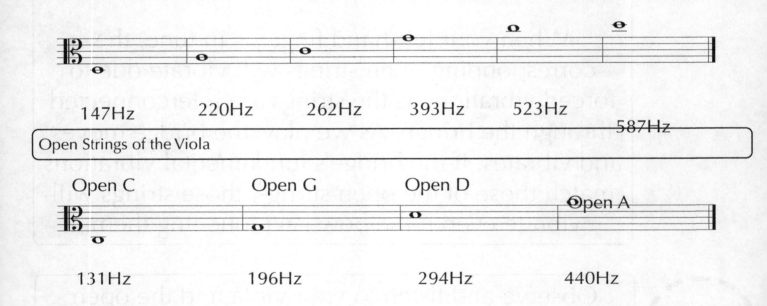

147Hz   220Hz   262Hz   393Hz   523Hz
587Hz

Open Strings of the Viola

Open C   Open G   Open D
                                        Open A

131Hz   196Hz   294Hz   440Hz

Observe the numbers. Can you spot any patterns or interesting facts? (*In this example, numbers are rounded, so the math is not exact).

When you play 1 on the C string, it produces a D note with vibrations of 147 Hz. If you multiply 147 by 2, you get 294 Hz, which is the open D. If you multiply 147 Hz by 3, you get 441 (440) Hz, which is the open A. Although it might be difficult to see, if your 1 on the C string is in tune, both open D and A strings should vibrate due to forced vibrations. You can actually see and hear the open strings and their forced vibrations.

Playing 1 on the G string produces an A note with vibrations of 220 Hz. If you double this frequency, you get 440 Hz, which is the open A string.

The vibrations of an open C string are 131 Hz, and if you double that frequency, you get 262 Hz, which corresponds to placing three fingers on the G string to produce a C note. So, when you press your ring finger on the G string, the open C string should vibrate. The same is true for placing the third finger on the D and A strings.

8. Quiz - new time signature and forced vibration

1. True or False. Cut Time has a different sum of the measure in 4/4 time?_____

2. What interconnects all the strings on the viola? The _____.

3. The sound of the viola is created by _____ of the string, which travel through the _____ and make the viola vibrate changing air pressure and creating sound.

4. What is the vibration expressed as a number of the open A?_____

5. What does Hz stand for?_____

6. How can a string vibrate if it is not plucked or bowed? Because of _____

9. Muscle tension and awareness

Muscle tension isn't always bad! Without it, we wouldn't be able to breathe, stand, walk, or play the viola. In order to create movement, our muscles use tension to contract and then relax.

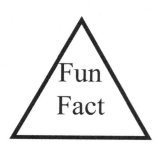

Our body has around 600 muscles!
Each muscle and muscle group performs different functions. Our job is to train them to do what we want, such as instructing our fingers to apply pressure and hold the viola and bow, or telling our shoulders to relax so we can move our hands.

Part III - Meaning in music and sound manipulation

10. How do we create meaning with sound?

Have you noticed that the way we speak changes drastically with different moods?

When we're really happy, we speak quickly or shout loudly and with a higher pitch in our voice. When we're sad, we speak much more slowly, quietly, and with a lower pitch.

When irritated, we tend to speak with very short and accented words.

When speaking or making music, such as playing the viola, meaning is conveyed by the quality and attributes of the sound. Loud, soft, fast, slow, high, low, smooth, or abrupt sounds all create different meanings in what you are trying to express.

Let's do an experiment

When different words are stressed or emphasized in a sentence, the meaning changes. Look at this simple sentence: "What are you doing here?" Read the sentence out loud, saying the word or words that are capitalized much louder.

1. "**WHAT** are you doing here?"

2. "What **ARE** you doing here?"

3. "What are **YOU** doing here?"

4. "What are you **DOING** here?"

5. "What are you doing **HERE**?"

Version 1, we want to know for what purpose someone is here: WHAT are you doing here?

Version 2, we want to know what activity someone is doing here: What ARE you doing here?

Version 3, we want to know why that person is here, and not someone else: What are YOU doing here?

Version 4, we want to know details of what activity someone is doing here: What are you DOING here?

Version 5, we want to know why someone is here, and not over there, or somewhere else: What are you doing HERE?

The meaning of each sentence can be further nuanced by changing how loud and how fast we say it. If we say sentence 1 in a slow and quiet tone, it's friendly. If we say the same sentence really fast and loud, it sounds angry and demanding.

The quality of sounds (pitch, speed, loudness, etc.) creates the meaning of the sounds.

11. Sound formula - learning to manipulate sound with the bow

Producing a beautiful sound on a viola is not magic, nor is there a secret formula. The viola is bound, like everything else, by the laws of science and physics. For us to learn how to change the sound, we need to have a fundamental understanding of what elements to change.

RULE!

The sound created by the viola is a result of:

Bow Resistance (pressure) x Bow Distance (length) x Bow Speed

There are 3 main elements responsible for creating a particular sound with the bow: bow resistance, or how much pressure the bow is applying to the string; bow distance, or how much bow you are using (half, quarter, or full bow); and bow speed, or how fast or slow the bow is moving.

By changing these elements, the sound produced by the viola will be altered.

You can think of the resulting sound as a formula. If you give each element a number, let's say 1-10, you can create different kinds of sounds, with 1 being the least and 10 being the most.

Let's create a formula for sounds and notes you already know, for a song played at a medium slow speed (walking speed Andante), and with quarter notes that mimic each step, for Twinkle Twinkle Little Star.

The song is played with quarter notes only. If you want to play softly or quietly, your formula will look something like this:

Sound = 3 Bow Resistance x 5 Bow Distance x 5 Bow Speed.

If you want to play loudly, your formula will look like this:

Sound = 7 Bow Resistance x 10 Bow Distance x 7 Bow Speed.

TRY

Play Twinkle Twinkle, Jingle Bells, Old MacDonald, and Lightly Row, but change your sound formula each time.

Play with full heavy bows, then fast light half bows... experiment and have fun.

12. Professional style bowhold

Mastering the professional-style bowhold will significantly enhance your control, and you'll find it easier to play once you get the hang of it. While it might be a bit more challenging than the beginner-style bowhold, where the thumb rests on the silver, the sound you produce and the control you gain are worth it. Be sure to check out page 55 in book 1, which teaches you how to perfect a beginner bowhold.

Let's start with the beginner bowhold:

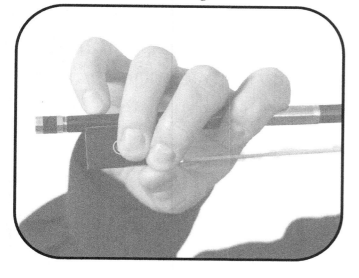

Keep your thumb square.

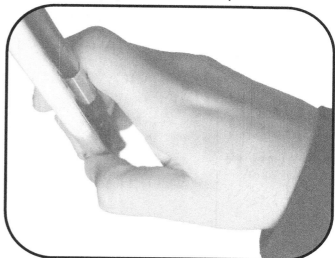

Position your thumb next to the frog.

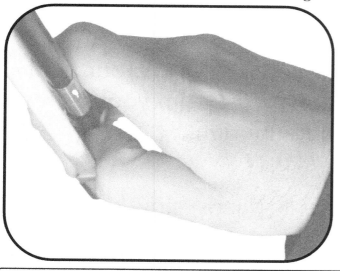

Important Information

Keep your thumb square at all times.

- The nail of your thumb should be just a breath away from the bow hair.
- Never rest your thumb inside the frog. Instead, place it next to the frog.

♪   19

One very strange concept to understand is how to change bow speed.

To play with a faster bow, you must use less effort and have less muscle tension. It is essential to learn how to let the right hand move more quickly with less muscle tension.

When we try harder, our muscles tense up, not allowing our hands to move faster.

Proper bow motion exercise: Move your right hand without the bow, wrist from your belly button to the right.

Do this with different speeds, slow to fast.

Try the same motions with the bow.

When you feel confident, try to play on open strings, and change your bow speed.

14. Bow resistance (pressure)

What really matters when playing with the bow is the interaction the bow has with the string.

The bow is a spring under tension. When the bow pushes on the string, the string pushes back on the bow. Newton's third law of motion states that every action has an equal and opposite reaction. When the bow applies pressure to the string, the string applies pressure back. The more pressure from the bow, the more pressure the string applies back on the bow. We call this bow pressure or resistance.

Let's learn how to apply pressure/resistance with the bow to the string.

Place the bow somewhere in the lower half (between the frog and the middle of the bow) on the string without moving it. Apply pressure to the string and feel how the more you press the bow on the string, the more the string will push back on the bow.

TRY

Bow on the string with NO resistance

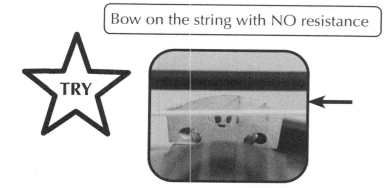

Bow on the string with light resistance

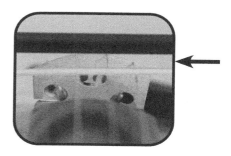

Bow on the string with medium resistance

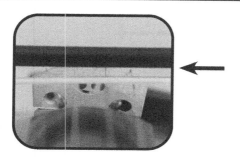

Bow on the string with heavy resistance

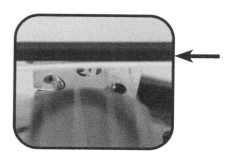

Most of the time we play with medium bow resistance/pressure

Bow distance and bow speed are not the same thing. You can play with fast short bows and slow long bows.

Important Information

We can play with half of the bow, in different parts of the bow, such as the upper half, lower half, or somewhere in the middle of the bow.

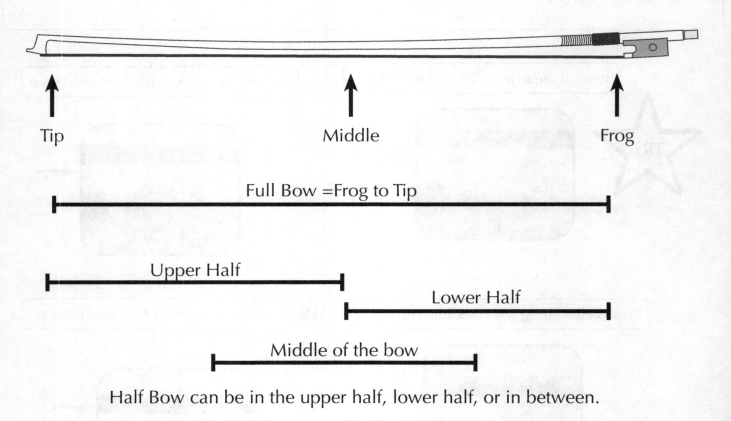

Tip

Middle

Frog

Full Bow =Frog to Tip

Upper Half

Lower Half

Middle of the bow

Half Bow can be in the upper half, lower half, or in between.

At Tip

At Frog

TRY

Play songs and pieces you know in different parts of the bow. Twinkle Twinkle in the upper half, Jingle Bells in the lower half.

16. Quiz - meaning in sound and sound manipulation

1. Meaning in sound is created by which qualities? _____

_____.

2. When we are excited and happy, we tend to speak _____.

3. When we are sad, we tend to speak_____.

4. Which word would you have to say louder in the following sentence if you wanted to make sure everyone knows that you want a giant toy?

"I want the biggest toy pony for my birthday"_____

5. The Sound Formula has three elements. They are _____,

_____, and _____.

6. To play as loud on the viola as possible you would have to use a lot or a little bow pressure?_____

7. True or False. Playing with full bow means, playing from the frog to the middle of

the bow?_____

The pinky, or fourth finger, is quite handy when we want to avoid moving across a string for a single note, only to return to the original string. Remember that open strings usually sound louder than notes played with a finger. So, in a sequence of notes played with a finger, an open string note may stand out because it's noticeably louder. However, we can prevent this by using our pinky for that one note.

Your pinky can produce the same note as the next open string. Look at the diagram below to get a clear idea of where your pinky should go. When you spot the number 4 above or below a note, it's a signal for you to place all four fingers on the fingerboard.

Consider this:

- If two notes are on the same string, use your pinky instead of the open string. This strategy helps you avoid switching strings just for one note.

- If the note before and the note after are on different strings, it's best to use an open string.

- Generally, when moving up, opt for open strings. On the way down, use your pinky, not open string!

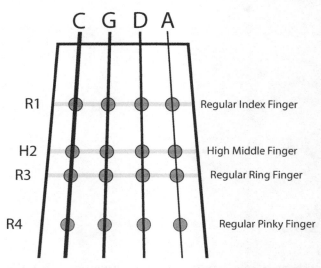

18. Developing fluency on the C string

a.

b

c

d

e

f

g

♪ 25

l Practice starting and stopping the bow gently.

19. Down and Up bows (bow direction)

Since we can play from the frog to the tip, or from the tip to the frog, we must name bow directions. This is especially important when playing in large ensembles with many members, as everyone's bow direction should match.

Down bows move with gravity, and thus are naturally slightly stronger and louder than up bows that move against gravity. As such, we usually play the first (strong/down) beat or note of the measure with the down bow and we play weak beats (up beats) with up bows.

Important Information

Safety is also an important concern. Viola bows are long and sharp, and if bow direction is mismatched when sitting close together, you run the risk of poking someone.

Down bow symbol

Up bow symbol

Does the bow actually move up and down when we play? Only slightly on the A string. Most of the time, our bow goes out and in, or right and left.

20. Retakes (lifts)

When you see a comma above a rest or a note, that indicates a retake. A retake is when you lift the bow in the air and bring it back to the frog without touching the string. This technique is often used during rests, to make sure that strong beats (down beats) are played with a down bow.

Retake (bow lift) symbol
Often used to play with down bows on down beats

21. Clair de la Lune - French Folk Song on C string

22. Flower Drum Beats of Fang Yang - An Hui Folk Dance (China)

23. Good King Wenceslas - Welsh Folk Song

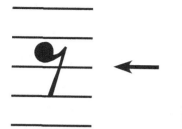

Eight Rest
Half a beat of silence

Eighth Rest   Quarter Rest

Both a slur and a tie are curved lines. They connect notes by placing notes on one bow. Any notes under a slur (curved line) must be played on one bow.

Each slur (curved line) means that all notes under one slur must be played on one bow. A tie, on the other hand, connects two notes of the same pitch and indicates that they should be played as a single, sustained note with the combined duration of the tied notes. In the example above, each bow gets two notes.

RULE!

Slur - Notes must be different

Tie - Notes must be the same. A tie simply makes a note longer by tying it together.

Slur - notes are different   Slur - notes are different   Tie - notes are the same

Often, ties are used when a note needs to be long, but not enough beats are left in a bar. The solution is creating a longer note with a slur across two or more bars.

Play the following exercises
Be sure to look at your bow and play with slurs as indicated in the music

a.

b

c

d

e

f

♪ 31

26. Dotted rhythm

One of the most challenging rhythms to play is the dotted rhythm.

Dotted rhythm is exactly what it sounds like, a note with a dot (period) on the side of it.

RULE!

A dot on a side of the note adds half of the note's value.

$$\circ \cdot = \circ + \text{♩}$$

$$\text{♩} \cdot = \text{♩} + \text{♩}$$

$$\text{♩} \cdot = \text{♩} + \text{♪}$$

$$\text{♪} \cdot = \text{♪} + \text{♬}$$

27. Exercises with dotted rhythms

♪ 33

The reason why notes with dots are so challenging to count is because the extra time/beats are invisible.

Important Information

The reason why notes with dots are so challenging to count is because the extra time/beats are invisible.

Tip: On the dotted quarter notes, make the dot the beat.

Beats   1+ 2   + 3 + 4 +   1+ 2   + 3 + 4 +

a

b

c

29. Ode to Joy, L. v. Beethoven - on C string, slurs, and dotted rhythm

♪ 35

30. Quiz - bowing techniques, slurs, ties, and dotted rhythm.

1. The pinky finger is used most often to avoid doing what?_____

2. The pinky on the G string makes (Note/Letter)_____what note?

3. Draw a down bow symbol_____

4. Draw an up bow symbol_____

5. True or False. The bow physically moves up and down when playing most strings?_____

6. What does retake mean? What does the bow have to do? _____

_____

7. Draw a retake symbol_____

8. Draw an eighth note rest_____

9. If one beat is a quarter note, how long is an eight note _____

10. What does a slur do?_____

11. Draw a slur_____

12. What is the difference between a slur and a tie? In a slur, the notes must be

_____and in a tie the notes must be _____.

13. What does a dot on a side of a note do and by how much?_____

14. How many beats would a half-note and a dot be? _____

15. How many beats would a quarter note with a dot be?_____

Legato in Italian means smooth.

Important Information

To play smoothly, make the changes in bow direction as effortlessly as possible. For a smooth bow direction change, try to keep the bow resistance and speed the same while changing your direction.

Staccato, in Italian, means separated. In order to separate sound, our bow must either fully stop, or the sound formula must decrease enough for there to be a large enough sound change to be produced, or to have the effect of creating a separated sound.

RULE!

Staccato does not mean short

To play with separated sounds, the bow must stop, and the note must be made shorter to create space, silence, or a decrease in sound; however, staccato does not mean short. Very often, you will have to separate medium length notes such as quarter notes, but you will still use at least half of the bow. The notes must be made shorter, to accommodate silence or decrease in sound for the separation, but the notes cannot be drastically altered and be made into much shorter notes such as sixteenth notes, in place of quarter notes.

To separate notes, the bow must either come to a full stop, or there must be enough decrease in bow pressure, speed, and distance (think sound formula) for the sound to be less and thereby perceived as a separation.

Gently stop the bow on each note.

You know to separate each note because there are dots below or above the notes.

Review page 22, line l, you practiced gently stopping the bow during the rest. Apply the same skill for staccato below (separation of notes by stopping the bow gently during the slur).

Important Information

Not all dots are the same.

Dots on a side of a note make it longer.

Dots below/above a note make it separated.

32. Review on the G string exercises

Optional exercises to work on intonation, muscle tension and awareness, posture, bowhold, sound production, and tone.

♪ 39

33. Bow distribution

Focus your attention on the bow and where you play. Bow distribution refers to which part of the bow a certain note or passage is played on. Long notes will typically get full bows, and shorter notes half bow.

34. Developing fluency on the on the G string - rests, slurs, dotted rhythm, staccato.

a.

b

c

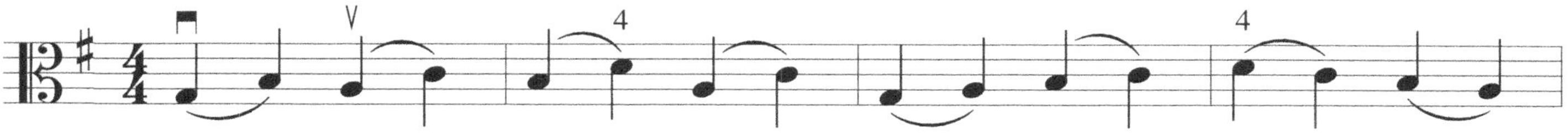

d

e

f

g

♪ 41

i Remember to gently stop the bow

j

k

l

m

m Challenge! Try to figure out why this exercise is so difficult?

35. Flower Drum Beats - Chinese Folk Song - G string

36. Clair de la Lune - French Folk Song on D string

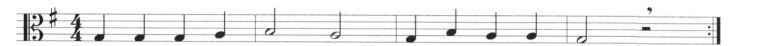

37. Good King Wenceslas - Welsh Folk Song on D string

38. Ode to Joy, L. v. Beethoven - D String

39. Dynamics

Dynamics tell us to play music either loudly or softly (there are many more, but we will focus on two core ones for now)

Important Information

f - *forte* (loud)
p - *piano* (soft)

If you recall section 2, the sound formula will help you to figure out how to play loudly and softly.

To play loudly, use more bow distance (use more bow), bow speed, and bow resistance (pressure).

To play softly, use less bow distance, bow speed, and bow resistance.

40. Crescendo and diminuendo

To make our playing more interesting and to have more meaning in our music, we play either louder and softer.

Crescendo means to get louder. By using more bow resistance, distance, and speed, you can gradually (little by little) increase the volume of sound.

Sometimes, you'll see the words cresc. written in the music. It means the same thing, to get louder. A hairpin, the word cresc. both mean the same thing.

Diminuendo (or Decrescendo) means to get softer. By using less bow resistance, distance, and speed, you can gradually (little by little) decrease the volume of sound.

Sometimes, you'll see the words dim. written in the music. It means the same thing, to get softer. A reversed hairpin, the word dim. both mean the same thing.

In any of the pieces or exercises, you can add your own dynamics.

41. Exercises on D string with diminuendo, crescendo and dynamics

Write your own dynamics, crescendos and diminuendos for the following exercises.

♪ 45

h

i

j

k

l

m Challenge! Use bow speed and/or bow placement to avoid getting stuck at the tip of the bow for l, m, n

n

42. Exercises on the D string with slurs, staccato, and dotted rhythm

a.

b

c

d

e

f

g

♪ 47

Bow challenge, try with full bows, half bows, lower half, upper half, gentle and strong bow separations.

h

i

j

k

l

m

n

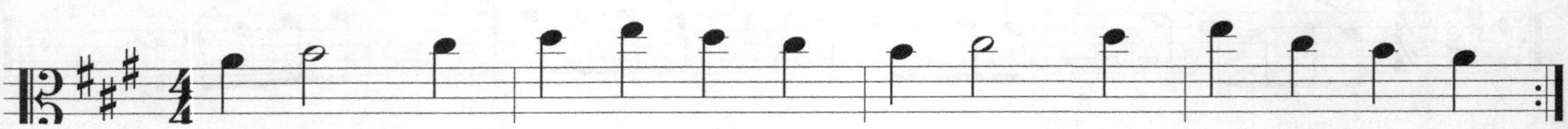

43. Flower Drum Beats - Chinese Folk Song - D string

44. Clair de la Lune - French Folk Song on D string

45. Good King Wenceslas - Welsh Folk Song on D string

46. Ode to Joy, L. v. Beethoven - D String

♪   49

47. Accents and tenuto

An *accent* is an attack or a bite at the beginning of a note. It looks like a sideways up bow. It is usually used to literally accentuate the note, and make it more important than the others around it by making it louder, especially at the beginning. To accomplish this, more bow pressure is applied at the beginning of a note and the bow is moved quickly while releasing bow pressure.

Have you ever touched something really hot? The way you quickly move your hand away from a hot object is very similar to how we play accents. Bite and release.

Tenuto is another technique used to bring out a note. Unlike an accent, tenuto brings out the note in a much smoother way. It literally means to emphasize the note. The best way to do this is to give the note a little more bow resistance/pressure and bow speed. This way it will sound louder, but not in an abrupt and sudden way as with an accent. Often, tenuto also means to sustain the note to its full length.

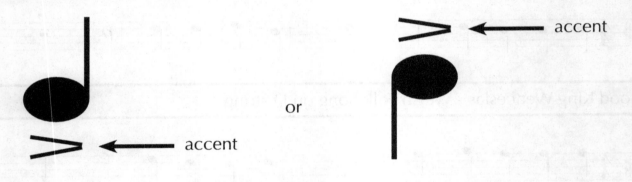

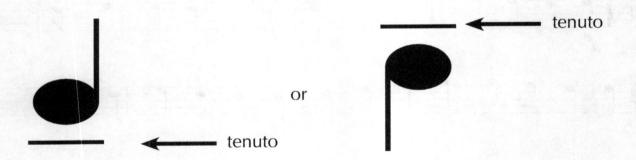

48. Fluency on the A string with accents and tenutos

♪ 51

49. Exercises on the A string, combining bow techniques

a.

b.

c.

d.

e.

f.

g.

♪ 53

h

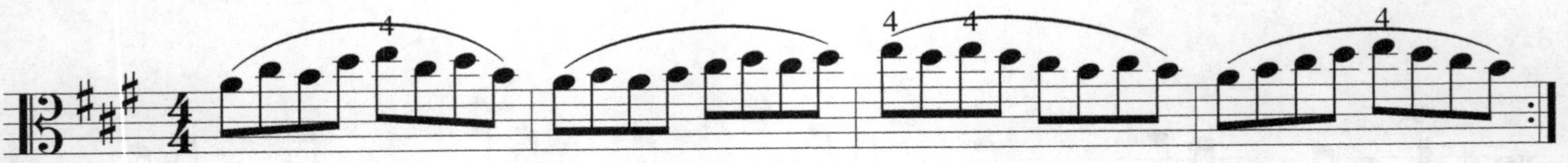

i

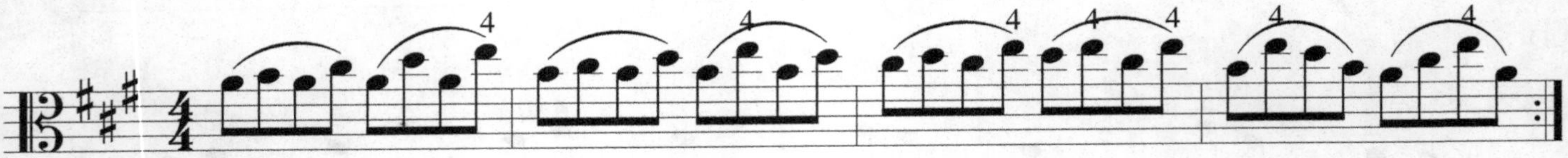

j

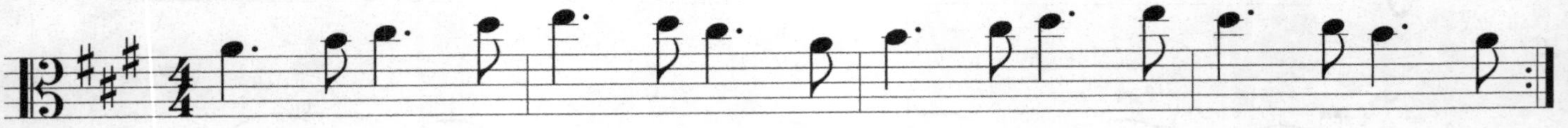

k

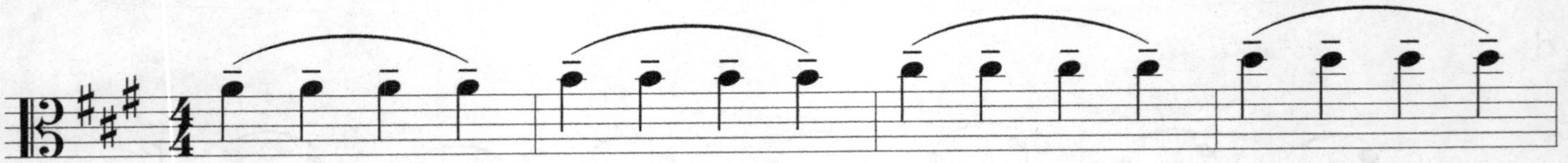

l

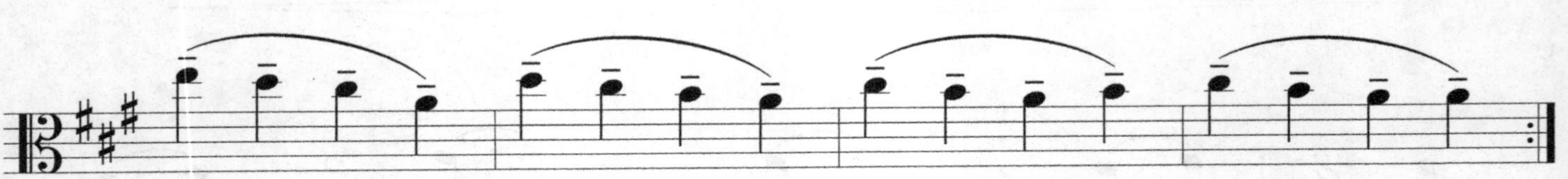

m

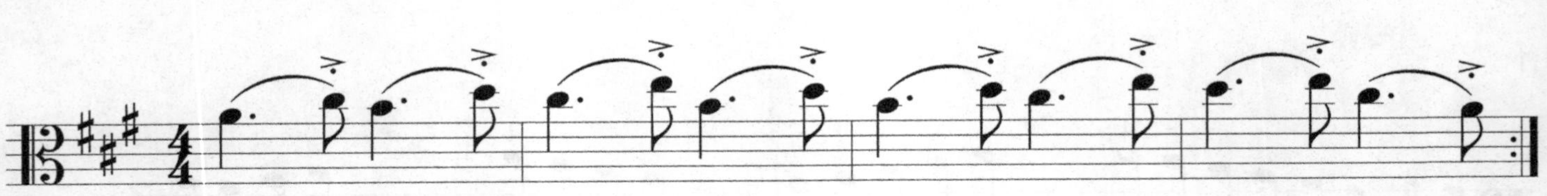

n

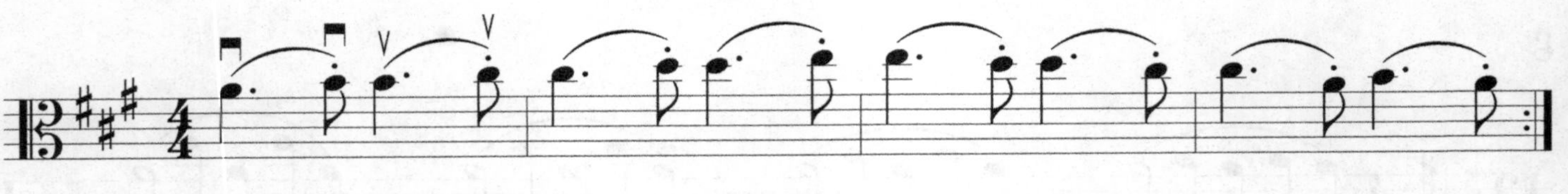

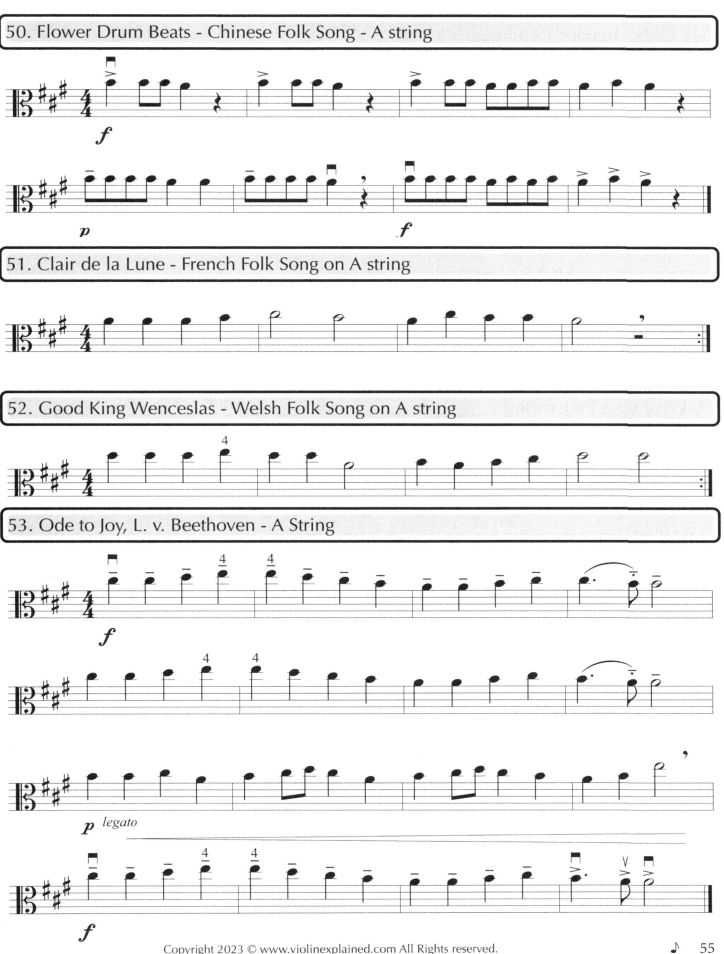

50. Flower Drum Beats - Chinese Folk Song - A string

51. Clair de la Lune - French Folk Song on A string

52. Good King Wenceslas - Welsh Folk Song on A string

53. Ode to Joy, L. v. Beethoven - A String

54. Quiz - Bowing techniques

1. What does legato mean?_____

2. How do you change the bow smoothly? By keeping the bow _____ and the bow _____ the same.

3. What does staccato mean?_____

4. How do we create staccato with the bow?_____

5. True or False. All dots are the same, whether they are on top, bottom, or the side of the note? _____

6. What does the word dynamic refer to? The length of the sound or the loudness of sound?_____

7. What does forte mean?_____
8. Write the symbol for forte._____ _

9. What does piano mean?_____
10. Write the symbol for piano._____ _

11. What does crescendo mean? _____

12. How do you play crescendo with the bow?_____

13. What does diminuendo mean?_____

14. How do you play diminuendo with the bow?_____

15. What is an accent? _____

16. Draw its symbol_____ _

17. How do you play an accented note? What does the bow have to do to create the accent?_____

18. What does tenuto mean? Draw its symbol_____

19. How do you play tenuto with the bow?_____

Part IV - Pieces with String Crossing

55. String Crossing Exercises - C and G strings

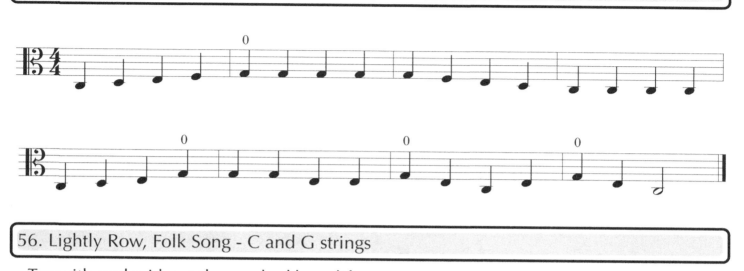

56. Lightly Row, Folk Song - C and G strings

Try with and without the marked bow lifts

57. Frere Jacque, French Folk Song - Exercise

58. Frere Jacque - French Folk Song

59. Go Tell Aunt Rhody - American Folk Song

60. Twinkle Twinkle Little Star, French Folk Song, lyr. Jane Taylor - D and A strings

61. Preparation Exercise for Song of the Wind

62. Song of the Wind - American Folk Song

63. Repetitive String Crossing on G and D strings

♪ 59

TRY Try writing in your own dynamics, *crescendos, diminuendos, accents,* or *tenutos.* Be creative, create your own meaning.

64. French Folk Song

65. Long Long Ago - T. H. Bayly

mf

f   *p*

mf

66. Retakes and up bows exercises

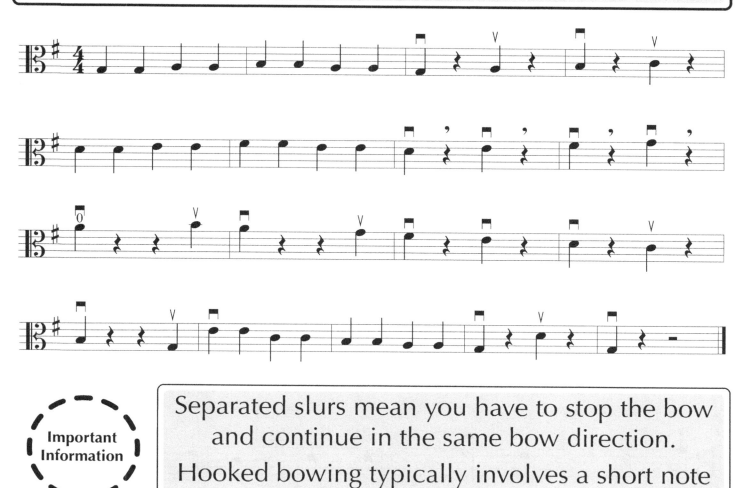

> **Important Information**
>
> Separated slurs mean you have to stop the bow and continue in the same bow direction.
>
> Hooked bowing typically involves a short note that is hooked to a long note.

67. Separated slurs and hooked bowing

68. Boat Song - Korean Traditional

Quick and Lively ♩ = 140

Part V - Low 2s Learning New Left Finger Placements

70. Viola Left Hand Map

Please review Book 1 Part 7. We use 7 different core note names (ABCDEFG) and we have 12 sub-divisions between low A and high A. We fill in missing subdivisions with sharps and flats, by making the string shorter or longer. The map below represents all the possibilities of where you can place your fingers on the viola. Although there are other ways to spell certain notes, we will focus and use the ones you'll encounter in music most often.

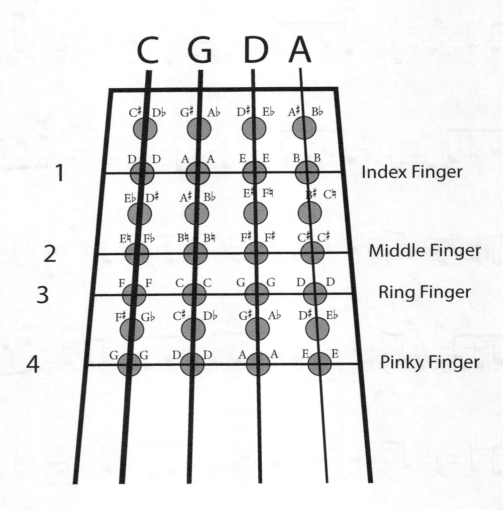

71. Introducing Left Finger Placement - L2 (Low 2)

Let's dive into learning how to play with a Low 2. You'll find that the Low 2 is just a half-step away from the first mark, which is where your index finger goes.

High or Regular 2 (Peace)

Low 2 (Squeeze)

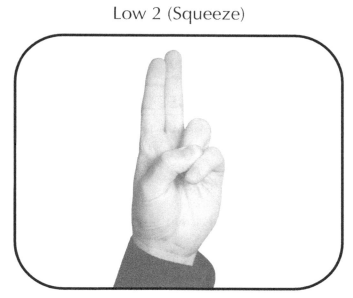

High 2 in Guitar Style

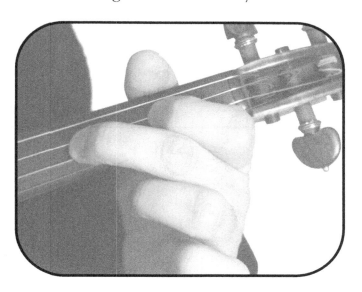

Low 2 in Guitar Style

High 2 in Proper Position

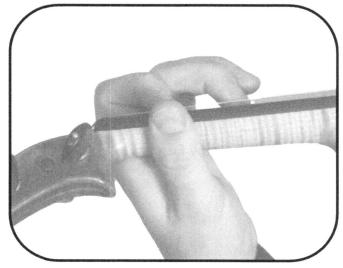

Low 2 in Proper Position

Remember to keep your index finger (1) in place on the tape while your middle finger (2) moves between the high and low positions!

Let's try playing: D (open) > R1 > H2 > R3 (keep your fingers on the marks).

Now let's play: D (open) > R1 > L2 > R3 (your fingers should be on the marks, but your 2 should be next to your index finger).

Keep your 1 pressed down on the string, bring your 2 close to it, and stretch your 3 out!

When you're using low fingers, they have a tendency to pull everything downward. After placing your Low 2, make sure to stretch your 3 and listen for the forced vibration.

72. Left Hand Map - C Major (Featuring Typical Low 2's)

We have a hand map for C major down below. You'll notice that High 2's are on the C and G strings, while Low 2's are on the D and A strings.

The next section incorporates both Low 2's and High 2's. You'll find an example for C major below.

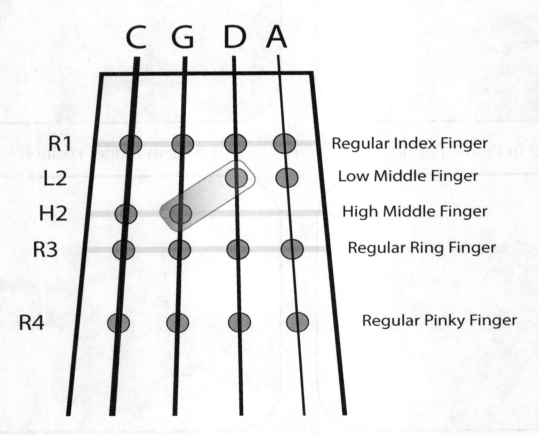

73. Low 2 Exercises on D string

74. Low 2 and slurs on A string

75. C major scale - 1 Octave.

76. C major scale - 2 Octaves

77. The Happy Sad Piece - Sergei Panov

♪ 69

Part VI - Familiar Songs with Low 2's

78. Dreidel, music by S.E. Goldfarb, Lyrics by S.S. Grossman

Moderato

79. Old MacDonald, American Folk Song

Allegro

80. Twinkle Twinkle Little Star, French Folk Song, lyr. Jane Taylor

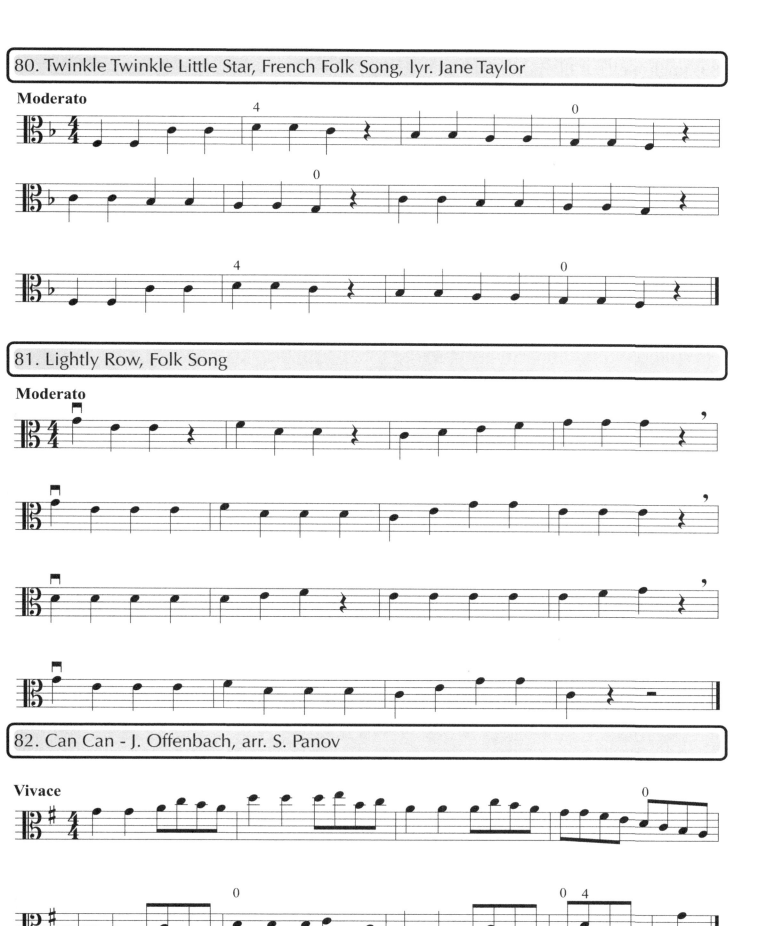

81. Lightly Row, Folk Song

82. Can Can - J. Offenbach, arr. S. Panov

83. Jingle Bells, J. Pierpont

Allegro

84. Ode to Joy - L.v. Beethoven, arr. S. Panov

Andante

Part VII - Triplet Eight and Quarter Notes

Soon, you will have to play eighth and quarter note triplets. A half note gets two beats, and its fraction representation is 1/2, which is a rational number. But you can also divide the sum of 2 beats (the half note) into 3 equal parts, creating triplets. Since a third (1/3) is an irrational number, the rhythm will feel off the beat because of the odd or irrational subdivision of time.

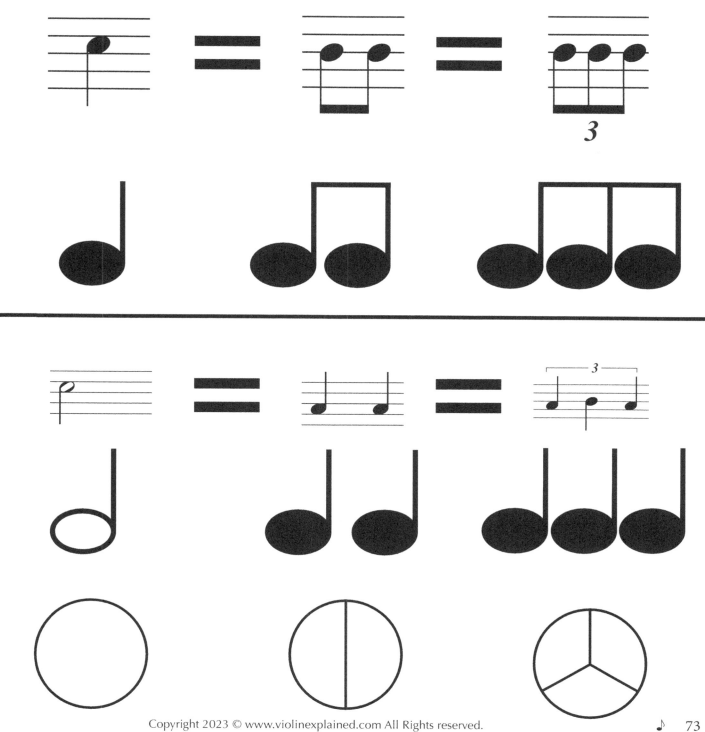

♪ 73

85. Eight Note Triplet Exercises - S. Panov

a.

b

c

d

e

f

g

h

i

j

k

l

m

♪ 75

86. Quarter Note Triplet Exercises - S. Panov

a.

b

Repeated string crossing is one of the most challenging bowing skills to learn. Playing the viola is a mentally intense activity, and naturally there is a tendency to use excessive muscle tension preventing efficient and effective motions, making repeated string crossing very difficult to execute accurately while keeping muscle tensions at proper levels.

TRY

Hold your right wrist with your left hand. Move your right hand up and down, left and right, and in circles clockwise and counterclockwise.

Now try the same exercise with the bow.

Important Information

When playing crossings between two strings, often we think that the wrist needs to move more. While that does help sometimes, technically it's not correct.

If we are playing repetitive string crossings, our right hand that holds the bow is pivoting at the right wrist, and it's actually the hand and fingers that move in circles, not the wrist.

Try the following exercise and see if you can make your right hand pivot at the wrist.

Grab right hand wrist

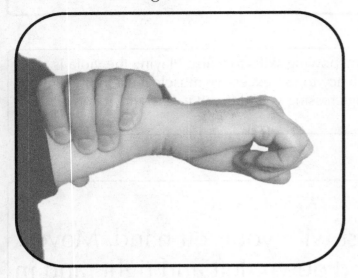

Wrist Up

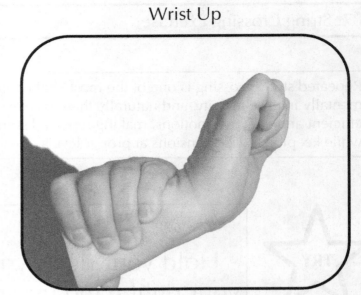

Wrist Right

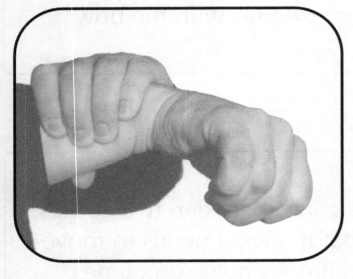

Wrist Down

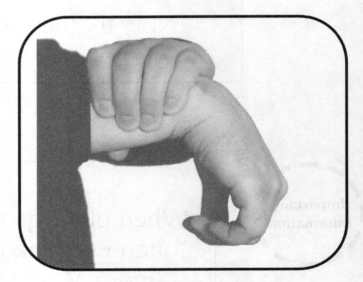

Wrist Left

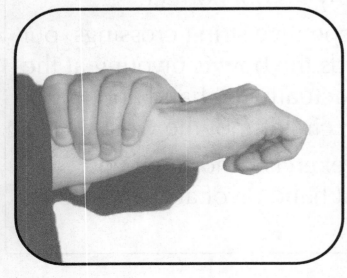

Repeat (Wrist Up...)

Now with the bow	Wrist Up
Wrist Right	Wrist Down
Wrist Left	Repeat (Wrist Up...)

While holding the viola

Wrist Up

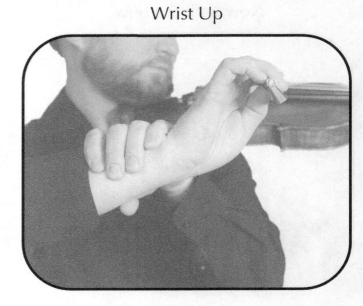

Wrist Right

Wrist Down

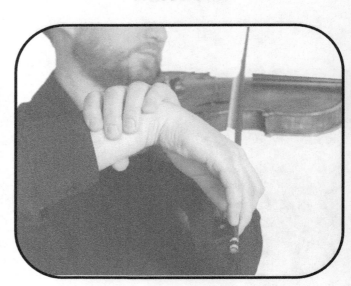

Wrist Left

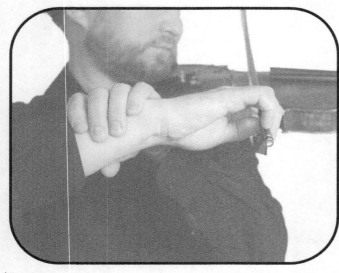

Repeat (Wrist Up...)

Part VIII - New Pieces with Low 2's

88. Playing Outside - S. Panov

89. Lost Toy - S. Panov

90. Hooked Bowing in 4/4 Time - S. Panov

91. Hooked on French Folk Song

92. Oh Well - S. Panov

93. Nobody Knows the Trouble I've Seen - American Spiritual

94. No Time but Triplet Time, S. Panov

95. Happy Birthday, Patty and Mildred J. Hill

96. We Shall Overcome - American Gospel Song

97. Oh My Darling, P. Montross

♪ 85

Jana Gana Mana

99. Liberty - American Hoedown

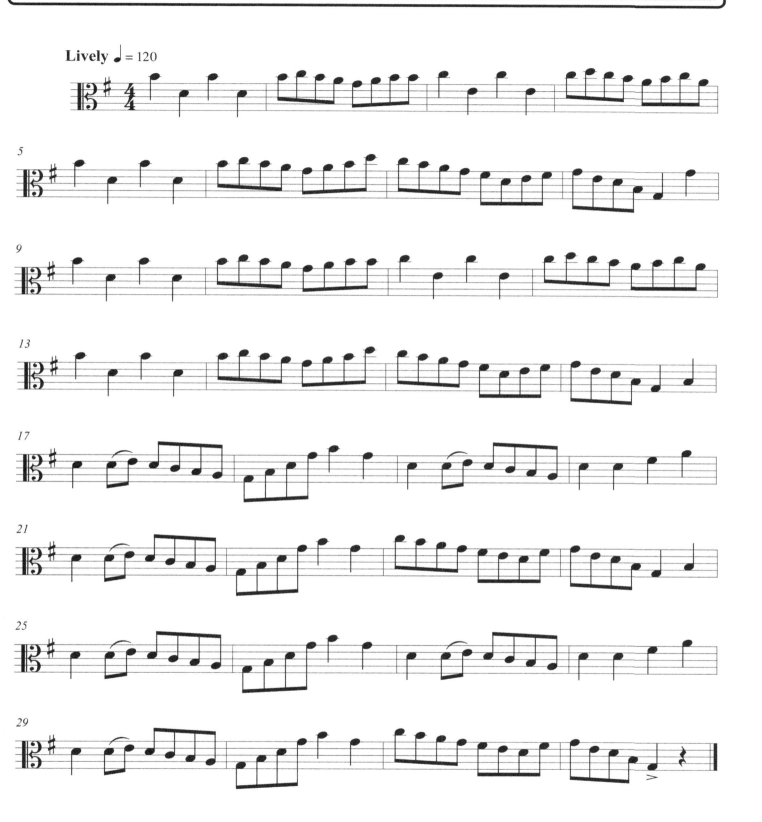

♪ 87

This space is left blank so the bass part on the right corresponds with the melody part on the left.

101. Minuet I - J.S. Bach - Bass

♪ 89

102. Minuet II - J.S. Bach - Melody

104. Battle Hymn of the Republic - W. Steffe

Moderato

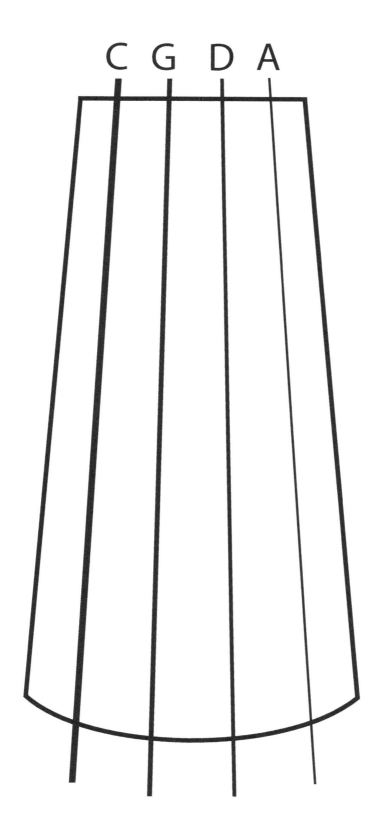

Photographer - Jessica Priscilla Caceda

Jessica Priscilla Caceda is a portrait photographer based out of Bloomfield, New Jersey. Jessica went to Gibbs College and has an Associate's degree in graphic design. Her passion for photography started in high school when she borrowed her father's Minolta camera for an elective class in photography. Since then, she's taken portraits of family and friends and eventually started attracting regular clients allowing her to create and establish her own business.

Jessica is Ecuadorian-American and speaks English and Spanish fluently. She's a new mom to a baby boy and lives with her husband Carlos. They enjoy traveling the world and eating delicious food wherever they go!

Instagram: jessica_priscilla_photo

Made in the USA
Las Vegas, NV
14 December 2023